T0072587

By the Same Author

Etre Soi-même. Genève: Poésie Vivante, 1967.

Rule of Life. Geneva: Poésie Vivante, 1969.

Lightning. New York: Vantage Press 1970.

Reflections/Réflexions. Bloomington, IN: AuthorHouse, 2004. (Various texts in English, French, and Arabic)

A Speech to the Arab Nation. The East/the West/the Arabs: Yesterday, Today and Tomorrow, and Related Writings. Bloomington, IN: AuthorHouse, 2007. (Text only in Arabic)

To Be Oneself: The Tragicomedy of an Unfinished Life History. Bloomington, IN: AuthorHouse, 2008.

Language teaching materials

Arabic Language Course, Part One/Cours de langue arabe, 1ère partie. 2nd ed. Genève: Poésie Vivante, 1979.

Arabic Language Course, Part Two/Cours de langue arabe, 2ème partie. Geneva: The Author, 1979.

Arabic Grammar/Grammaire arabe. Genève: The Author, 1979.

Arabic Elementary Course, Volume One/Cours élémentaire de langue arabe, volume 1. Genève: The Author/Poésie Vivante, 1982.

Arabic Elementary Course, Volume II (Annexes)/Cours élémentaire de langue arabe, volume II (annexes). Genève: The Author/Poésie Vivante, 1983.

Handwriting Exercise Book/Cahier d'écriture. Genève: The Author, 1984.

Dialogues Textbook I: Words of Everyday Use/Manuel de dialogues I: vocabulaire courant. Genève: Institut d'enseignement de la langue arabe/Poésie Vivante, 1984.

Dialogues Textbook II: United Nations, Questions and Answers/Manuel de dialogues II: Les Nations Unies, questions et réponses. Genève: Institut d'enseignement de la langue arabe/Poésie Vivante, 1984.

Dialogues Textbook III: Words of Everyday Use/Manuel de dialogues III: vocabulaire courant. Genève: The Author/Poésie Vivante, 1985. (Suite au Manuel I)

Nacereddine's Multilingual Dictionary: 2500 Arabic words of current usage with translation in 7 languages - English, Français, Español, Deutsch, Russkij, Chinese, Japanese. Geneva: The Author, 1991.

Alphabet illustré. Genève: The Author, 1996.

Arabic Pictorial/L'Illustré arabe. Geneva: The Author, 1996.

Chinese Pictorial/L'Illustré chinois. Geneva: The Author, 1997.

Russian Pictorial/L'Illustré russe. Geneva: The Author, 1997.

Interactive Arabic/Arabe interactif. Geneva: The Author, 2004. CD-ROM.

The Multilingual Pictorial Dictionary: Arabic, Chinese, English, Français, Español, Deutsch, Russkij, Japanese. Geneva: The Author, 2011. CD-ROM.

Fundamental Arabic Textbook/Manuel d'Arabe fondamental. Rev. ed. Bloomington, IN: AuthorHouse, 2008.

A New Approach to Teaching Arabic Grammar. Bloomington, IN: AuthorHouse, 2009.

Nouvelle approche de l'enseignement de la grammaire arabe. Bloomington, IN: AuthorHouse, 2009.

The Illustrated Multilingual Dictionary: English, Français, Español, Deutsch, Russkij, Chinese, Japanese (Text, Image & Sound). Geneva: The Author, 2011. CD-ROM.

Manuel d'écriture et de prononciation arabes. Bloomington, IN: AuthorHouse, 2011.

Handbook of Arabic Writing and Pronunciation. Bloomington, IN: AuthorHouse, 2011.

Publications used in the United Nations, Geneva, Arabic   Language
Courses - not UN official publications

*Grammatical Applications: Idioms and Locutions of Everyday Use/Applications
grammaticales: idiomes et locutions d'usage courant.* Geneva: 1980.

*Arabic Language Course: Practical Exercises/Cours de langue arabe: exercices
pratiques.* Geneva: 1981.

Livre de conversation, première partie. Genève: 1981.

*A Dictionary of International Relations (news-economics-politics)/Dictionnaire des
relations internationales (actualités-économie-politique).* Geneva: 1986.

A Basic Dictionary: Everyday Vocabulary/Dictionnaire de base: vocabulaire courant.
Geneva: 1987. 2 v.

A New Approach to Arabic Grammar. Geneva: 1988.

Nouvelle approche de la grammaire arabe. Genève: 1988.

Handwriting and Pronunciation Handbook/Manuel d'écriture et de prononciation.
Genève: 1991.

For further information, please visit
www.a-nacereddine.com

Abdallah Nacereddine

Words of Wisdom

A Collection of Verse
Philosophical Introspections, Maxims and Aphorisms

2nd Edition, revised and enlarged

authorHOUSE®

AuthorHouse™ LLC
1663 Liberty Drive
Bloomington, IN 47403
www.authorhouse.com
Phone: 1-800-839-8640

© 2012, 2014 Abdallah Nacereddine. All rights reserved.

No part of this book may be reproduced, stored in a retrieval system, or transmitted by any means without the written permission of the author.

Published by AuthorHouse 07/01/2014

ISBN: 978-1-4772-6644-1 (sc)
ISBN: 978-1-4772-6645-8 (e)

Library of Congress Control Number: 2012916273

Any people depicted in stock imagery provided by Thinkstock are models, and such images are being used for illustrative purposes only. Certain stock imagery © Thinkstock.

This book is printed on acid-free paper.

Because of the dynamic nature of the Internet, any web addresses or links contained in this book may have changed since publication and may no longer be valid. The views expressed in this work are solely those of the author and do not necessarily reflect the views of the publisher, and the publisher hereby disclaims any responsibility for them.

Introduction

I started remembering events only when I was about six years old. It was in 1945, at the end the First World War, when the French army invaded our farm located far away from our village, where my great-uncle lived with his family. They were looking for him. Fortunately, he was not there. They arrested his two young sons and took them to headquarters for interrogation, and then they let them go. They were furious at not finding their father. They did not do any killing. However, they started shouting, just to scare the population around. As soon our family and other relatives heard the news, together with the inhabitants of the village, we took what we could of our belongings and getting ready to flee, seeking refuge up the mountains. Fortunately, the army did not come. I relate this event in detail because of the profound effect it had on me. Although it happened sixty-seven years ago, I vividly remember it as if it happened yesterday. From that event on, I started to remember everything, but nothing prior to it. For this reason, some acquaintances who read my Autobiography, To Be Oneself: The Tragicomedy of an Unfinished Life History, were amazed at the way I related some events and described some scenes that happened in my childhood and later on so distinctly.

It was as if I was sound asleep, and that event shook me and woke me up. I have heard or read that a person can remember something he/she did, or that was done to him/her, or any other important event as early as the age of two and half years. Therefore, it was unusual for me not to remember any-thing before I was six years old. Whatever had happened, I guess I repressed it, because it was too painful to remember on a conscious level. There were some events I wish I remembered, and others I wish I did not. But a person cannot choose what to remember and what not to. Apparently, according to psychologists, our subconscious mind makes the selection for us, for our own good, so it reasons what to remember and what to repress. It may be too painful to remember some things, but they affect us, nonetheless, throughout our life, whether we are aware of them or not. As Alfred Adler stated, "By the time a child is five years old his attitude to his environment is usually so fixed and mechanized that it proceeds in more or less the same direction for the rest of his life. His apperception of the external world remains the same. The child is caught in the trap of his perspectives and repeats unceasingly his original mental mechanisms and the resulting actions." [1]

As I already mentioned, the subconscious mind prevents us from re-membering some happenings in our early childhood in order to protect us from suffering. Perhaps it is also the other way around: remembering those happenings may heal us, as proven by hypnotherapists. When they make their patients remember things they have repressed, they make them feel better. Just like when we hear a noise, not knowing where it comes from, or loud talk in a restaurant, for example: as soon as we look around and get acquainted with the source, we feel less disturbed by it.

I never knew what these repressed things were. No one said anything

viii

about them, and I did not ask. Yet I was constantly reminded by family members, relatives and neighbors of my 'Words of Wisdom', so to speak, which I used to utter at a very early age, that is when I was four or five years old. What I said was not some amusing, childish, witty words, but something very wise and solemn. I can tell from the way they remind me of them, the way they repeat them to themselves or to others. For me, what I was saying was just ordinary talk. For others, however, they were words of wisdom. Several times friends or members of the family reminded me of things I said over forty years previously.

They were adopted as rules to abide by. There were several sayings. Unfortunately, there are no records of them. It is obvious that in an illiterate society nothing was written. Everything was related, transmitted only orally. It never occurred to me to record them, of course not as a little child, nor even as a teenager, since I was illiterate like everyone else. Very often, teenagers keep private diaries where they record everything happening to them. The most renowned diary of a teenager was Anne Frank's. When I was in the army, I was in charge of the library. We had books in Arabic and French. Of course, like everyone else, I heard all sorts of proverbs in Berber, Arabic and French at that time, but I did not have in the library, nor had I come across a book elsewhere of thoughts, maxims, aphorisms, written in one single book by some writer, thinker or philosopher.

I had to wait to be twenty-seven years old to find out about that kind of book, such as:

Pensees – Blaise Pascal. Translated by W.F. Trotter. Oxford: Benediction Classics, 2011.
Maxims – La Rochefoucauld. Translation, introduction and notes by Stuart D. Warner and Stéphane Douard. South Bend, IN: St. Augustine's Press, 2009.
Thoughts of Marcus Aurelius. Seattle, WA: CreateSpace, 2012.

Among the books I read on mainly Western philosophy – that was in 1966 – those three books encouraged me to start recording my thoughts and reflections. One day, I remember I said something, which came to my mind right at that minute, to one of my colleagues in the restaurant where I worked when I was a student. As soon as he heard it, he was so affected that he went immediately around repeating it over and over to all the other co-workers. Another co-worker would have behaved differently. What one finds sensible in what I have said, another would find senseless. In general, people react in different ways to what they hear and see. Not only different people, but also the same person, react differently, depending on the mood they are in.

Even though my knowledge of French was not very advanced, I managed to write a considerable number of maxims of my own for compilation in a little book. Finally, my dream came true. I published the book. It was certainly not a best seller. Very few people bought it. Nobody took me seriously. Up to now, each time I say something about my book Reflections (texts in English, Arabic and French), people ask me, "Are they quotations from other books?" or, "Are they quotations from the Koran?" At the beginning, I was offended, and then I became so used to that reaction that it did not bother me any longer. Fortunately, there were a few people who accepted them as coming from me and were deeply affected by them.

In Japan it was fabulous. I had four remarkable friends. They were much older than me when I met them. First I made acquaintance with Dr. Kanji Hatano, who was the rector of the O-chanumizu University. He introduced me to Professor Hiroshi Sugo, who was a Professor and Director of the Kindergarten at the same university, and Mr. Hiroshi Miyazaki, Secretary-General of the Institute for Democratic Education, who introduced me to his friend Professor Kato, a retired science professor. All of them read my writings in French and English. They were very moved by them. They did not ask me, "Are they quotations from Shinto or Buddhist scriptures?" They immediately started to translate them, make comments on them at length and publish them in different literary reviews. Thus they made my writings known all over Japan [2]. That was in 1970 and 1971. The little books in question were:

Etre Soi-même. Genève: Poésie Vivante, 1967.
Rule of Life. Geneva: Poésie Vivante, 1969.
Lightning. New York: Vantage Press, 1970.

xi

These books are now out of stock. In any case, I consider that several thoughts expressed in them are not valid any longer. However, some of them are still valid, so I thought it would be worth-while reproducing them in another book, which I published in 2004, that is thirty-four years later. I added some fresh writings to them, and published them under the title Reflections. Lately, my writing style has changed somewhat. All my thoughts started to come to me in couplets. They come spontaneously, without forcing, but not without reason – each one has a story behind it. They have always been generated after an event or during meditation and contemplation. That could be at anytime, anywhere. Some of them are related to each other, others are not. Each couplet stands by itself, and can be read separately. In the first pages, I clearly use the first person singular pronoun 'I'. When I subsequently use the first person plural pronoun 'we', and the second person pronoun 'you', I very often mean 'I'.

They deal with various topics. The book has no table of contents. The only way to know what the subjects are is through the Index.

For twelve years after I set up my website in 1998, I had no idea whether it was visited or not. However, since August 2010, I have started getting detailed statistics of visitors every day. As of August 2012, the site contains several hundred pages on various subjects. They are all visited from time to time. Among the most consulted are the pages I entitled Words of Wisdom in three languages: Arabic, English and French. They were mainly in Arabic, at the very beginning. One of them, particularly, Words of Wisdom-Arabic (6), was the most visited, when I only had a few pages. It consists of seven couplets. It is no wonder that it became a universal anthem. I was really delighted, but I was not at all surprised because I know the reason why. This verse happened to have something from each of the following: Tao Te Ching (Taoism); Bhagavad-Gita (Hinduism); Buddha's doctrine (Buddhism); Psalm 23 (Old Testament); the Lord's Prayer (New Testament); the Koran and Hadith (Islam) and from the Hellenistic philosophy of Zeno of Citium (334-262 B.C.) (Stoicism).

It is obvious that I am deeply affected by all these great world religions and philosophies to which I am very grateful.

Later on, I added a few pages in Arabic and French, and a considerable number in English, each containing around six couplets. Each page is visited from time to time. Amazingly, some of them in different languages are visited daily from different cities of 167 countries in five continents: from China in the East to the USA in the West; from Norway in the North to South Africa in the South, as well as from all the countries of the Arab World: from Kuwait, in the Middle East, to Morocco, in North Africa, as well as from Islands in the Atlantic, Indian, and Pacific oceans, and the Caribbean.

It is not really interesting to know whether my website is visited or not, but what is interesting and impressive is realizing that there are still many people who are looking for peace and wisdom in a semi-mad world where violence reigns. Another interesting phenomenon I notice daily is that visitors from different continents, i.e., far from each other, happen to visit the same pages of Words of Wisdom at different hours of the same day, given the time difference, and, amazingly, sometimes simultaneously. It means that people, whoever, whenever and wherever they are, could communicate constantly telepathically, relate and are linked to each other by the Universal mind.

Because of the success these 'Words of Wisdom' have on the Web, I was encouraged to publish them in their entirety in a book, available for all, for those who have access to Internet, and those who do not.

Geneva, June 2014   Abdallah Nacereddine

---

1. Ansbacher, Heinz L.; Ansbacher, Rowena R., eds. The Individual Psychology of Alfred Adler. New York: HarperPerennial, 1964, p. 189.
2. See Nacereddine, Abdallah. To Be Oneself: The Tragicomedy of an Unfinished Life History. Bloomington, IN: AuthorHouse, 2008. Chapters; Tokyo, Japan (1) and Tokyo, Japan (2).

I must explore and exploit 1
This gold mine of mine, 2
As well as this oil well, 3

I have hidden in my mind. 4
Or else, I will explode. 5

Whether I like it or not, 6
That, for sure, is my lot. 7

I have no other alternative, no other choice, 8
Except to listen carefully to my inner voice, 9
And accept myself just as I am and rejoice. 10

1

I sure am influenced by my readings, being a great reader,   11
But I'm no one's follower, nor am I some kind of a leader.   12

If I were a leader, I would not want, by any means, to get all the blame   13
For the atrocities my followers would eventually perpetrate in my name.   14

I do not intend to make with my writings any profit,   15
Nor do I claim that I could be some kind of prophet.   16

I no longer want to be right. I seek to become strong,   17
For when I am mighty, I am right, even if I am wrong.   18

I prefer to be wrong   19
In my own sight,   20
Rather than to be right   21
In the eyes of the throng.   22

When I was a child I was different. I was regarded as a holy boy. I was very lonely.   23
If only I were an ordinary child, I would have been happier. I did not want to be holy.   24

I was not flattered. One can well imagine   25
How desolate I was, living on the margin.   26

I talk only when it is necessary. I do not speak out of caprice.   27
I either teach, preach, prophesy, or keep quiet, hold my peace.   28

I was known by my roommates   29
And likewise by some intimates,   30

To be a student who lives   31
On bread, milk and olives.   32

It's obvious that my contribution to human welfare is but a little drop in the sea.   33
That is right, but the sea is made of all little drops put together, you would say.   34

3

Why do bad things happen to good people 35
And make them suffer, and so turn purple? 36

That is the price to pay to make them good. 37
That's why they ought to be in a good mood 38

In spite of them, whether they like it or not, 39
They can do nothing about it; it is their lot. 40

It sure only takes a few good words 41
To make us well and heal our wounds. 42

At times, you may feel desolate and empty as a deflated balloon. 43
You're in union and communion with everyone. You're not alone. 44

4

When things fall apart. When you fail in everything you undertake, and feel let down. 45
When things are bad and cannot get worse, they sure get better. It's dark before dawn. 46

No matter how you suffer, do not despair. Everything comes and goes. It is the norm. 47
Nothing goes on forever. Happiness and suffering alternate. It is calm after the storm. 48

Be courageous. Never give up hope. For a long time nothing seems to happen. 49
All of a sudden, you see the light at the end of the tunnel, and doors start to open. 50

Nothing goes on forever. It's dark before dawn. After darkness, you see the light. 51
Everything comes and goes; joy and suffering alternate just like day and night. 52

No matter how somber the night, you know that the next day the sun will shine. 53
Everything's a flux. No matter how many hardships you suffer, you will be fine. 54

However desolate, remain connected, keep in touch; do not be withdrawn. 55
Be strong. Pull yourself up whenever you feel as if you were going to drown. 56

Keep alert, do not wander off; don't become distant.   57
Live in the present moment, in the very instant.   58

Some of us may have all they need to be happy, living in the present instant.   59
Yet, we feel miserable, reliving some painful past traumas, however distant.   60

You don't feel good. You have been through this before. You survived. You'll be okay.   61
Every disease has a remedy. Every problem has a solution. Every locked door has a key.   62

You may fall ill and physically feel weak. With age the body cannot help but decay.   63
Yet you keep up your morale, no matter how you suffer physically, spiritually you feel okay.   64

When you become sick, don't be so sad. Bear with it. You have no choice.   65
When you recover, you will feel better than before. So you must rejoice.   66

Sometimes you think that something is damaged forever, but it only needs repair.   67
Just as there sure is a way out when you are stuck. There is no reason for despair.   68

Whenever you despair, you say, this time I'm stuck forever. Then you discover   69
To your amazement, it was only a temporary situation, not meant to last forever.   70

We often worry unnecessarily. We expect the worse to happen. So, what's the remedy?   71
To be more positive, to expect good things to happen, to turn a tragedy into a comedy.   72

You deal with any situation, bear your suffering, and confront your hardship   73
With serenity. You take charge of your life. You're the captain of your ship.   74

At times, you go from one crisis to another. You think you're going to have a fit.   75
However, whether you admit it or not, very often, it is all for your own benefit.   76

We believe there must be a reason for this pain   77
And have a firm belief that it is not all in vain.   78

For sure, with might and main   79
You shall overcome your pain.   80

Only by knowing the origin and causes of our suffering, using our brain, 81

Will we heal ourselves. We shall not let all our hopes go down the drain. 82

When you suffer so much you can't help asking yourself, 'What is all this suffering for?' 83

The answer soon comes when you recover and find you are feeling better than before 84

When stricken by pain, don't let yourself be overwhelmed by it, however severe. 85

It will pass. If it lingers, you go on resisting until it subsides; you persevere. 86

Miracles do happen. One can happen to you after all these years. 87

You shall overcome all your fears and shall no longer shed tears. 88

When one gets mad at you, don't be vengeful. Instead be kind to him. Don't forget 89

That something or someone else may be bothering him. 'You are not the target.'(1) 90

When one hurts you, do not hurt him back. Say peace. 91

And you sure won't fall apart, but remain in one piece. 92

(1) You Are Not the Target.
A book title by Laura Huxley. Farrar Straus & Giroux (T); Third Printing edition (June 1963).

Hate and revenge make your condition worse. It would not do you good to inflict 93
On others what you suffered. Only love and forgiveness can resolve your conflict. 94

No matter whom, what and for whichever reason you hate, you sure will suffer. 95
For your well-being you have to love, you must have something better to offer. 96

Being vengeful doesn't resolve your conflicts. It makes you feel more resentful and bitter. 97
You do realize that only by being forgiving and compassionate would you feel better. 98

No matter how hurt, don't hold a grudge. That makes you suffer more. It's healthier to forgive. 99
Keep on repeating 'I forgive' until you really feel at peace. Not only an impression you give. 100

Even if you think it's impossible at the beginning, say 'I forgive'. Repeat it often. 101
In retrospect, you will be amazed. Without realizing it, your heart will soften. 102

You went through many hard times, yet you survived. There is no hardship you can't withstand. 103
You don't deny your pain. You face it. You don't, like an ostrich, stick you head in the sand. 104

9

When you are assailed by an evil thought, acknowledge it, in spite of feeling bad.   105
Do not deny it. It's a disease. Heal it. Do not repress it. Do not hide under the bed.   106

You must know everything, the whole truth, however tougher,   107
However unbearable, about yourself, and, if necessary, suffer.   108

Rather than living the unconscious life of a cheerful idiot,   109
Nor do you allow yourself to lead a life on automatic pilot.   110

Don't take medicine unless necessary. Healing through prayer and meditation,   111
With no side or after effect, is more preferable to treatment with medication.   112

We think we can do nothing about destiny. Yet we can change our predestination,   113
As we can change our mind about going somewhere, by changing our destination.   114

When you observe yourself attentively, you may find some things bizarre.   115
Acknowledge them. While you work hard to improve, accept yourself as you are.   116

10

When you uncover something unpleasant about yourself, do not say that it is not me. 117
Accept it as a part of you. Heal it and befriend it. Do not regard yourself as an enemy. 118

When you undertake an action, don't ask whether or not you will succeed. 119
Likewise, you don't ask whether it will grow or not when you plant a seed. 120

You certainly do not expect to get rid of all your pain. 121
You are realistic; you sure don't build castles in Spain. 122

Whenever one hurts you, you will not hurt him back. 123
And say nothing either to his face or behind his back. 124

If you ever want to say something to someone, you say it to his face. 125
You do not say it behind his back, for sooner or later, it will surface. 126

You cannot hide something forever. Sooner or later it will surface. You won't say a lie. 127
You're gentle with yourself and with everyone else. You do no harm. You won't hurt a fly. 128

11

No matter how unkind a person is to you, you do no harm; you will not lay a finger   129
On him. After calming down, you'll be happy to not have been carried away by anger.   130

No matter how hurt you feel, you choose not to act and keep silent.   131
Because if you react and talk, you may lose control and be violent.   132

When you hear an argument, do not be too impulsive in making comments.   133
If you have to, think about what you should say and wait a few moments.   134

When hurt, you may show your 'claws,' something you cannot prevent.   135
But you do not use them to 'scratch' anyone in retaliation, in any event.   136

Acknowledge your failures, but don't feel sorry for yourself. Don't dwell   137
On them. Do focus on many other things that you can do very well.   138

When you are in need, you feel a strong urge to receive.   139
Likewise, when you have plenty, you feel an urge to give.   140

12

Be good, gentle, but not weak. Be strong, but not arrogant.   141

Be thrifty, but not miser. Be generous, but not extravagant.   142

Do not lower yourself, but be elegant.   143

Be solemn, dignified, but not arrogant.   144

Be careful not to keep making the same mistakes. But there is no need to repent.   145

Do your best to be thriftier, instead of feeling sorry for the money you have spent.   146

If you want someone to forget what you have said to him, just say nothing. That is it.   147

Because if you tell him 'forget everything I said', he certainly will do just the opposite.   148

Unless necessary, say nothing about other people. It sure will be reported.   149

Whether good or bad talk, what is reported could very often be distorted.   150

If you want no one to know what you do, don't do it. For sooner or later it will be known.   151

Just as, whether you like it or not, you cannot prevent from reaping what you have sown.   152

You have a choice to remain ignorant. But if you don't like what you learned, you may yearn   153
To become ignorant again. But you have no choice. What you learned, you cannot unlearn.   154

Be loving and lovable, but free. Do not be a slave,   155
Too attached to the person or to the thing you love.   156

If you are happy now because some man or woman loves you,   157
You know that you'll be sad if that man or woman leaves you.   158

You go to the end and persevere in any action you undertake.   159
Do not stop in the middle no matter how long it will take.   160

Let no one tell you how to behave. You need no guide.   161
Whether something is good or bad for you, you decide.   162

You act on your own. You follow no example. You need no reference.   163
You do what's right. Approved or disapproved of, it makes no difference.   164

14

You do what pleases you. You need no permission from anyone, no license.   165

Likewise, you no longer abide by anyone's rules. They make to you no sense.   166

You shall no longer be a yea-sayer. From now on you say 'no,'   167

Firmly and assertively, but calmly without acting like a volcano.   168

If one puts pressure on you, you simply ignore him. There's nothing you need to do.   169

You do not react. You keep very calm and cool. You do not turn into a tornado.   170

If you do not feel like talking and are asked a question, you do not have to reply.   171

Just as when you are often given very foolish orders, you are free not to comply.   172

You are not rigid, nor amenable. You are flexible, but only to a certain degree.   173

You don't approve of everything. You think things over; you agree or disagree.   174

You cannot satisfy but yourself by being righteous. All the rest,   175

What other people think of you, is not really of interest.   176

15

You cannot undo what has been done. Avoid doing it again. No need to be sorry.   177
In the future you won't make the same mistake. You'll even do better. Don't worry.   178

If you think that you do not need something, do not throw it right away with the trash.   179
Keep it for a while. It could still be useful. You can get rid of it later. There is no rush.   180

When you say I'll do it tomorrow, it'll always be tomorrow. You never do what you postpone.   181
Further, don't fancy someone will do it for you. You have no one except yourself to rely upon.   182

Don't leave till tomorrow what you can do today. You must only postpone suicide,   183
Day after day till you change your mind, as your wish to hurt yourself will subside.   184

You will be happy indeed   185
To be still alive, not dead.   186

There are things that once done are not possible to undo. All you have is sorrow.   187
Do not act impulsively when you're unsure of something. You wait till tomorrow.   188

16

When you are angry, say nothing, do nothing. In other words, do not talk, do not act.   189
When you come to your senses, you discover that that was not you, as a matter of fact.   190

No need to ask our point of view about things. One can tell from the way we look.   191
Happy, we see things beautiful; sad, we see them ugly. It depends on our outlook.   192

When we are joyful, we perceive life as rosy and in bloom.   193
When we are depressed, we perceive it as doom and gloom.   194

One day we believe that one thing is bad; the next, we think that it's good.   195
Things remain the same. They do not change. What changes is our mood.   196

When people say something unpleasant to you, it may not be their intention   197
To hurt your feelings. They may mean well. Forgive them. Don't pay attention.   198

What we hear and see could sometimes have on each of us a very different impact.   199
Though it's the same, we process it differently, That's revealed in the way we react.   200

17

It certainly is impossible to change the world, people and things. 201
One can change the way one perceives them and the way one thinks. 202

When we ruminate the past and anticipate the future, and say who knows what lies ahead? 203
We actually feel joyful or sad not because of what's going on in the world, but in our head. 204

You can't change people and things as to turn into bright what is dark. 205
In the same manner, you sure cannot make a dog meow and a cat bark. 206

You think that people smile or frown at you. It is not people; it is you. They only reflect, 207
Just like a mirror, what you feel inside yourself, whether it is peace, harmony or conflict. 208

When you lose your temper, you say one thing convinced that you're right, to discover 209
That you are wrong, when you are back to normal, come to your senses and recover. 210

No matter what the hardship you go through, your will stay unbroken. 211
So will your trust, confidence and faith in yourself remain unshaken. 212

18

You sometimes ache all over, overwhelmed with pain, stricken and shaken.　213
Rest assured, you're strong. You're only a wounded lion(ess), not a chicken.　214

Life is beautiful and the world is a safe place to live in, and it is propitious, not adverse.　215
No matter how unsafe you feel, you're protected by the Higher Sources of the Universe.　216

The world is no longer as it was years ago. But it's not going mad.　217
It is different. We can't change it. We accept it as it is being made.　218

When you live in harmony with all your environment, and are loving and loved,　219
You feel at ease, and all your problems and inner conflicts are being resolved.　220

You wouldn't change things. You let them take their course without interference.　221
You accept both of them: life and death; they are alike. You have no preference.　222

You don't have to be a somebody. You're loved unconditionally. Remember　223
You are worth just as you are, a human being, not a machine or a number.　224

Money is not everything. Even if you haven't got a cent, 225
You sure are great, if you're sensible, honest and decent. 226

You are able to overcome your difficulties and you will cope, 227
No matter the conditions, be brave. Never lose faith and hope. 228

You'll see the light at the end of the tunnel, and will not be at the end of your rope. 229
While there is hope there is life, and vice versa, while there is life there is hope. 230

You are all alone against all. You have no support whatsoever, no ally. 231
You can count only on yourself. There's nobody on whom you can rely. 232

Even if all your friends forsake you, you'll not be miserable. It will not be the end. 233
You will still be happy if you love and care for yourself. You'll be your own friend. 234

It is not because you are unfriendly, unsociable that you don't want to mix with the multitude. 235
It is because you are not afraid, like everyone else nowadays, to live with yourself in solitude. 236

To be or not to be with the crowd has really nothing to do at all with loneliness or solitude.   237
You can feel alone with people and vice versa. Loneliness is but a state of mind, an attitude.   238

There is nothing wrong with you. You are not strange. Do not be upset. Do not panic.   239
You are not like everybody else. You are different. You are special. Your are unique.   240

You fit nowhere. You are rejected. You are desolate, yet you must be proud.   241
You are special, unique, you're one in a million; you're not one in the crowd.   242

You don't have to be dressed like everybody else. You don't wear a uniform.   243
Just as you ought not to behave like the crowd. You do not conform.   244

With no doubt, we are amused by watching an actor play another person's role.   245
Yet, watching him play his own role in real life, would we still find him so droll?   246

You lack education; you are unskilled. That's all right. You do your best to improve.   247
But you do not owe anybody an explanation. You have absolutely nothing to prove.   248

21

There is really nothing in the hand of a selected few. All is within everyone's reach. 249
You have access to all you yearn for. You can be very knowledgeable and grow rich. 250

If you believe you'll succeed, according to the law of attraction, you attract success. 251
Dare to undertake any action to which you thought only a selected few had access. 252

When talking, pay attention whether you interlocutor is listening or not to you. 253
You don't talk in the air whether someone is listening to you or not, like a radio. 254

Be open to all teachings. Take what fits. You don't have to follow them to the letter. 255
So dare to undertake an arduous task. Do what you can now, and do the rest later. 256

Do not be influenced by talk that'd make you joyful or sad, 257
For, without thinking, people say things that are nice or bad. 258

Do not close your ears; listen to people but don't pay attention to everything they say. 259
Keep your eyes open. Look, but don't be too emotional, however painful, by everything you see. 260

22

You are not concerned about what people do or say to and about each other.   261
You don't hold yourself responsible for everything that happens to them either.   262

You're not protected when your life is threatened, and you feel very insecure.   263
Just as you are abandoned when you are ill, and are provided with no cure.   264

You sometimes get very depressed and feel pain from head to toe.   265
You've friends. But when you need consolation, there's no one to turn to.   266

You were under stress; there was violence all around you. You got scared.   267
You felt alone and desolate. You cried out for help, but nobody cared.   268

Being raised to be fearful as a child; as a grown-up you often get scared.   269
You may look fine on the outside, but on the inside you feel terribly scarred.   270

Don't ask anyone 'What can I do for you?' Just to defy you, they ask of you the impossible.   271
When they fail to do something, instead of blaming themselves, they hold you responsible.   272

23

You're in danger. You feel vulnerable, apprehensive, living in constant fear.   273
No one ever comes to your rescue; no one wants to get involved, to interfere.   274

From now on you're self-sufficient, self-reliant. You're co-dependent no longer,   275
As day after day you become more and more confident, stronger and stronger.   276

All men and women call you sister or brother.   277
When you're in trouble, nobody would ever bother.   278

In other words everyone naturally calls you brother or sister.   279
But no one rescues you when you run into something sinister.   280

You cannot prevent people from making you angry, but you sure can overcome anger   281
By changing yourself, by growing, becoming more and more confident, and stronger.   282

Do not be too self-centered, self-absorbed. Do not think of yourself only.   283
You may be more fortunate than those who are more afflicted and lonely.   284

24

Just as you look where you put your feet when walking,   285
You ought to be careful and mindful when you are talking.   286

You watch what you say. You do not repeat like a parrot   287
All those ready-made sentences you have learned by rote.   288

For many years we go on suffering, without knowing why. That is simply because   289
We look outside ourselves instead of inside. We don't realize that we're the cause.   290

Just as we look beforehand where we will end up, before leaping,   291
When we intend to plant a seed we first think of what we'll be reaping.   292

You live in reality. You do not fantasize, daydream.   293
Just as you go not against, but with the stream.   294

You'll overcome all obstacles. You'll break this iron curtain,   295
Which is standing in your way. You will succeed, for certain.   296

Let no one get in your way. Move on. Never stop   297
Until you fulfill all your wishes and reach the top.   298

Be persevering in your undertakings, no matter how long that takes.   299
Even if you do not succeed, you will still learn from your mistakes.   300

You ward off troubles with calmness and benevolence.   301
You sure do not generate them with anger and violence.   302

You react to anger not with anger, but with calmness. You will feel better.   303
You know that you certainly can't extinguish fire with oil, but with water.   304

When someone offends you for no reason, sometimes, you feel hurt.   305
But you do not hold a grudge against him. For you have a good heart.   306

He hurts you one time. You graciously forgive him, because you are so kind.   307
Misinterpreting you kindness, he hurts you again. He thinks you don't mind.   308

If you keep on being kindhearted to him even when he is mean to you, he senses 309

That you are more magnanimous and wiser than him, then he comes to his senses. 310

Some men are not so refined. It is no wonder that they behave like brutes. 311

Alas, they do not know any better. "Yea shall know them by their fruits." 312

When children fall, learning how to walk, they try again until they stand up on their feet. 313

As adults, when we fail to do something, we try again and again. We accept no defeat. 314

Children do not learn how to walk right away. They try again and again each time they fall. 315

We, as grown-ups, learn through trial and error. We do not easily give in whenever we fail. 316

You take delight in doing your job, not only for the money you are earning, 317

But for your contribution to the human welfare and the skills you're learning. 318

Your primary concern is to live with everyone in harmony. 319

That for sure is more important than having a lot of money. 320

When you do a good deed, do not expect any reward,   321
Not even to be thanked, neither immediately nor afterward.   322

When you accomplish a good deed, you do it for its own sake.   323
If you expect a reward and don't get any, you'll have a headache.   324

You ought to be   325
Just like a bee.   326

That is quite possible. A bee spends all its time making honey,   327
But doesn't expect to be thanked for its deed nor get any money.   328

Some people take great pride in being mean and nasty. That is too bad.   329
They do not know any better. One cannot give what one has never had.   330

When you are sad and mad, act as if you were happy and calm. You'll be tending   331
To feel really so in the final analysis, you'll see; not only feigning and pretending.   332

When you find it hard to do something, keep on doing it without cease.   333
Do not be discouraged. You will doubtlessly end up doing it with ease.   334

People may not take you seriously. Even when you solemnly say something, they laugh.   335
When you behave exactly the same way they do, they understand that enough is enough.   336

Live within your means. Don't be extravagant. And do your best not to borrow.   337
For there is no guarantee that you will be able to pay off your debts tomorrow.   338

You live within your means. You may lend money but you do not borrow.   339
Give but take only the money you have earned by the sweat of your brow.   340

Be generous. Remember, giving does not diminish you fortune. It makes it grow.   341
Nevertheless, don't accept money you haven't earned with the sweat of your brow.   342

You imagine people look down on you. You do your best to show your true worth,   343
In order to feel better, but that is all in vain. You only make your condition worse.   344

29

When you are asked to act against your will, you do not obey; you refuse   345
Nicely and gently; don't rebel. Gentleness is not weakness. Don't confuse.   346

Because of the inferiority complex instilled in some of us since our birth,   347
Whatever we do, we think that nothing that comes from us has any worth.   348

We never play lottery, which simply means to yearn   349
To get very easy money others worked hard to earn.   350

Men are all created equal, but one man shows what in him is the best.   351
Another prefers to behave, consciously or unconsciously, like a beast.   352

We are created equal. There is in all of us a human being and a beast. That's normal.   353
Yet we act differently. One man behaves like a human being, another like an animal.   354

You are great. Do not belittle yourself. Say, 'Big me.'   355
Do not say, 'Little me.' You are a giant, not a pigmy.   356

One's behavior has nothing to do with being a man or a woman, nor with education. I do find   357
Some uneducated people more courtly than the so-called educated ones, who are more refined.   358

What attract people is not the tree, but the flowers and the fruit it bears.   359
There're many people who have nothing to offer, of whom nobody hears.   360

There are subjects you would like to talk about and other things to share.   361
But there's nobody to talk to. Even if there were someone, you won't dare.   362

You participate in conversation. You don't just sit, listen and observe.   363
You carefully watch what you say. You express yourself with reserve.   364

Express yourself. You know the effectiveness of the word.   365
More than a deed, it can do miracles. It can change the world.   366

You think you have nothing to say. Start expressing yourself and ideas will flow. Like a tap,   367
Closed, nothing comes out of it. When you open it, water starts to flow. It does not stop.   368

31

Language is only a tool. Two people speaking the same language may not have much   369
To say to each other if they think and feel differently. Their viewpoints may not match.   370

You were made to be afraid of monsters, God, hell, Satan. That was not fair.   371
Rest assured. You're all safe and secure. There is nothing and no one to fear.   372

You wouldn't let yourselves get stuck, blocked.   373
You go ahead and open the door, if it is locked.   374

Sometimes you get so disgusted with yourself and life, you wish you had never lived.   375
However, when you think of some very good deeds you have done, you feel relieved.   376

Be conscious of what your body and mind are doing, But do not be too self absorbed.   377
Pay attention to other people; observe them. Do not forget that you are also observed.   378

You think before you say or write something, because all you say or write   379
May be used against you in the near or distant future, whether wrong or right.   380

32

You ought to think before undertaking any action, uttering any word, Be cautious.   381
You must always know what you mind and body are doing. Be aware, conscious.   382

Some people are averse to anything new, unfamiliar, as being strange.   383
They want things to stay as they are. They don't want them to change.   384

You may thank people in advance when they promise you something. But do not forget,   385
They may change their minds. Don't count on it. What you're promised you may not get.   386

When a man promises you something and doesn't keep his promise, you won't feel sorrow,   387
Knowing well that he is such a man who is deciding today what another will do tomorrow.   388

When one person promises you something, thank him for his intention, but it is no use waiting.   389
He may not keep his promise. He's one person promising for another. Waiting is time wasting.   390

One day he behaves like an angel, the next he turns into a devil. What a shame!   391
That is because he has two different personalities, which are not at all the same.   392

When you tell him that he has two personalities: one is good, the other is bad, 393
That one does not know how the other acts, he doesn't admit it, and gets mad. 394

You can't make his two personalities know each other by bringing them both face-to-face. 395
They don't exist simultaneously. When one vanishes, the other appears and takes its place. 396

Let that part of you that is civilized watch over the other part that's wild. 397
And let each grown up, mature part of you take care of your inner child. 398

What really interest us in man are not his beliefs, but the way he acts. 399
Neither does his talk interest us. What we do want from him are facts. 400

Man is never at rest. He's always moving, acting, communicating. He can't just be. 401
In other words, he cannot sit still, quiet, doing and thinking of nothing, like a baby. 402

Man is always chatting, moving about. Unless he is ill 403
He cannot just keep quiet even for a while, and sit still 404

For all you go through, you cannot always be cheerful. You might be sad. 405
But you are supposed to look jovial all the time, even if it's only a facade. 406

Don't give in to despair. Don't keep your heart down. Don't fall prey 407
To anxiety. Keep calm and relax. And as antidote meditate and pray. 408

No matter how serious your illness is, you will recover, for every disease there is cure. 409
However vulnerable, you won't be hurt, you live among friends, you're safe and secure. 410

What you are going through is reality, not only a nightmare, a bad dream. 411
No one pays heed to your pain nor does one hear you if you ever scream. 412

You face your hardship with calmness and serenity. You do not complain. 413
You don't talk about it either, because it is not something you can explain. 414

Your suffering is not something you can explain, 415
Because it may not be that easy, simple and plain. 416

Further, it is hard for the uninitiated to discern. 417
Besides, it is yours, and nobody else's concern. 418

Be patient. Your condition is improving. You soon will be all set. 419
Don't despair. There is really no reason at all for you to be upset. 420

Do not be upset, if you get no recognition from those you serve. 421
You sure will get from someone else all the reward you deserve. 422

We do not mock anyone hoping, thinking that he is but a diminished man, a lame. 423
Anything, good or bad, can happen to anyone, anytime. But nobody is to blame. 424

If we harm someone, who doesn't harm us back, let's not think we'll get away with it. 425
Someone else will sure make us pay for the wrong we have done. We will have a fit. 426

We won't let that happen in any event. We won't have a fit. Before we act 427
We think of the consequences. For this reason, we treat everyone with tact. 428

No matter how unworthy you feel, don't let yourself down. Don't sink.   429
You are useful. Rest assured, you have more potential than you think.   430

If you're a failure, people sympathize with you. They are sincere. But if you succeed   431
And do better than them; they'll hate you for it. There are limits you must not exceed. 432

You talk only when necessary. You do not waste your precious time with gossip and idle chat. 433
You are not talkative but active, productive. You do not just eat, drink, sleep, living like a cat. 434

A cat or a dog does not have to do anything to be loved, just like an idol.   435
But you, as a human being, cannot be loved by being unproductive, idle.   436

Similarly, you could be charming, cute, just like a doll.   437
That is not enough if you are not clever, if you are dull.   438

You reap what you sow. You are very careful in what you invest.   439
You realize that if you sow a good seed, you make a good harvest.   440

You certainly do not only seek your comfort, 441
Having everything without making any effort. 442

You face hardship with equanimity; you do not repress or express your anger. 443
You release it. "What doesn't kill you", says Nietzsche, "makes you stronger." 444

When you succeed, people say you're lucky. They're wrong. It has nothing to do with luck. 445
It's not lottery. It is faith in yourself, determination to succeed, either you have or you lack. 446

You are appreciated for who you are, not at all for what you have, 447
What you know or what you believe in. But for the way you behave. 448

When you plan to undertake an action, being convinced that it is the right thing, go ahead 449
And do it, with or without other people's approval. If they discourage you, do not pay heed. 450

When you intend to do something, go ahead and do it. Let none stand in your way. 451
People are not aware of what you are capable of. Don't come under no one's sway. 452

You don't shake even if you get a big blow, a knock.   453

You are unaffected; you remain steady like a rock.   454

You are doing fine. So, don't panic. Keep calm. Let go.   455

You soon will feel relief, no matter what you undergo.   456

What you are going through at present is enough. So why not just relax and let go?   457

You need not suffer from what had happened in the past, which was a long time ago.   458

Do not be too tight. Relax. Do not take life very seriously. It's all the same,   459

Whether you win or lose, succeed or fail in what you do, life is but a game.   460

You must not stop acting all together, simply because you make a lot of mistakes.   461

On the contrary, you keep on acting till you do things right, however long it takes.   462

When you fail in doing something, you go on, no matter how long it takes.   463

One learns through trial and error. Likewise, you learn from your mistakes.   464

39

Never let yourself be at a loss, nor get trapped and stuck. 465
That's when you can neither run away nor counter-attack. 466

When you find your goal very hard to achieve, don't give up. Don't abstain 467
From striving with all your might convinced it is something you will attain. 468

Don't work too hard. A man can die of something he overdoes. 469
In the same way, a drug addict could die from an overdose. 470

The way you feel, think, whether you are loving or hostile, 471
All's reflected and revealed in your demeanor and lifestyle. 472

You can tell whether a man does love you or he's just using you as a means 473
To fulfill his own desires, and what he says may not be what he really means. 474

We're made to follow precepts without questioning them and behave as we're told. 475
Most of them are all false, yet they seem genuine. But all that glitters is not gold. 476

For decades we held so many beliefs, and behaved just as we were taught. 477
Then we discover that those beliefs were all wrong, not as we had thought. 478

No matter how much you love your work, do not overdo it. So take a break, So I suggest. 479
Just as no matter how much you enjoy your food, you can't eat more than you can digest. 480

Although we fully take part in worldly things, we live with the strict minimum like a nun 481
In a convent or a monk in a monastery. We are not supposed to enjoy life and have fun. 482

Some of us cannot fully enjoy ourselves. All our life here on earth is a mere test 483
To determine our final abode: hell or paradise. Like it or not, we cannot protest. 484

We often feel ashamed and guilty for nothing. We ask ourselves, "Why this shame and guilt?" 485
The answer is: Shame and guilt are instilled in us since we were a fetus, they are inbuilt. 486

Everything's taboo. You don't dare to undertake any action from fear of committing a sin. 487
They made you believe in imaginary things that never existed and that nobody has ever seen. 488

41

You hesitate to act. Whatever you do makes you feel guilty. It's always the same scenario.   489
Rest however assured. You do everything right. You are not committing any sin. Are you?   490

When we make a mistake, we are not only rebuked and perhaps punished for it today,   491
We won't hear the end of it. We will be reminded of it again and again until we die.   492

We don't stick to beliefs our parents and teachers were instilling in us since we were born.   493
We change them if they are not right. We're flexible; we're not amenable nor stubborn.   494

Whether we admit it or not and regardless of our big differences, from what I gather,   495
We all have the same origin. Each one of us should be treated as sister and brother.   496

For our own good, we have no choice but to live in peace with each other.   497
If we're different "We scrape and polish one another until we fit together."(1)   498

"Hobble your camel", says the Prophet Muhammad, "and trust in God."   499
Do trust in God. But do not think of Him as if He were your bodyguard.   500

(1) Kant, Immanuel. Lectures on Ethics. New York:
Harper & Row Publishers, Inc., 1963, p. 198.

All men think they are omniscient, but they're uncertain; they grope,   501
"Our ignorance", says William James, " is a sea, our science a drop."(1)   502

You are only at your very beginning, but you go on. You don't stop.   503
"A thousand-mile journey", says Lao-tzu, "begins with a single step."   504

It had already happened several times, but you did find your way out.   505
In case it happens again, you will find your way out. There's no doubt.   506

All is in a state of flux, nothing remains for ever,   507
Just as "You cannot step twice in the same river".(2)   508

All the turmoil your mother went through during her pregnancy, before you were born,   509
You were unconscious of it. Yet it may affect you, and the traumatism is a fatal thorn.   510

Your subconscious registers all impressions while still in the womb. Although fetal,   511
They affect you all through your life, either for your own good or they could be fatal.   512

(1) James, William. Writings 1878-1899, New York. The Library of America, 1992, page 496.
(2) Heraclitus.

Some of us have been taught as children that every little mistake we made was a sin.   513
And made afraid of imaginary, non-existent things and beings no one has even seen.   514

Just as they instilled fear and guilt in us long before we were born,   515
And made us believe that if we disobey, we'll go to hell and burn.   516

We go on dealing with people although some of them don't tell the truth; they lie,   517
Yet we are convinced there are still some we can trust and on whom we can rely.   518

There's nothing to learn from them. All they want to teach you, you already knew.   519
It is always the same story. You have heard it a thousand times. It is nothing new.   520

Many a man thinks that he is perfect. It never occurs to him to ask himself, 'Who am I'?   521
Whereas he is always telling you who you are, and that you have 'a speck in your eye.'   522

You do want to tell them what you really think of them, to teach them a lesson.   523
They're not interested. They act is as if they were deaf, they don't want to listen.   524

44

They sure have eyes, but do not see. They have ears, but do not hear. 525
They live in the past and elsewhere, instead of living in the now-and-here. 526

For centuries most of us were enslaved to the false beliefs we were taught. 527
We accepted our fate. It was for our own good. How wrongly we thought. 528

It is not because somebody tells you that doing something is hard, that you resign, 529
Don't cling to acting in a certain way. If you don't succeed you find another design. 530

It is obvious that something must really go wrong with a man you see limp. 531
Apparently, he may seem all right, but he could suffer from a phantom limb.(1) 532

We are guided by the dead, whom we blindly obey, 533
Whose instructions however outmoded we abide by. 534

They're unconscious of all the harm they do. They have no feelings. They are careless. 535
They want things done their own way, whether right or wrong, they wouldn't care less. 536

(1) phantom limb, a sensation experienced by someone
who has had a limb amputated that the limb is still there.

45

They do not realize that you are as sensitive as they. That really shows 537
That they never put themselves in your or in any other person's shoes. 538

According to Freud, depression is sadness, anger, repressed, turned inward, not expressed. 539
They know all about your condition, but they could not care less. They are not impressed. 540

Most best-sellers are quickly written, published, read and quickly forgotten. They're junk literature. 541
That is what people like to read, just as they like eating junk food. We can't change human nature. 542

All that is offered is junk. The providers have no choice. They comply 543
To what people want to consume. It is a matter of demand and supply. 544

We offered them pearls, but they wanted onions. We are not shocked. We understood. 545
It is obvious they do prefer onions to pearls, because they can eat them. They're food. 546

That's the most natural. There's nothing new about this. Haven't you ever been told 547
What Heraclitus has rightly said a very long time ago, "Asses prefer straw to gold." 548

46

That is quite right, neither is gold worth straw nor a pearl worth an onion.   549
Straw and onions are both food for animals and humans, in their opinion.   550

In order to fill their stomachs with food by eating they prefer to cook,   551
Instead of filling their heads with knowledge by reading a good book.   552

That's why they say, in order to buy some groceries, "Let's go to a souk",   553
Instead of saying, "Let us go to a bookstore in order to buy a book."   554

One may fancy that he's loved. Then one day he discovers that he is despised.   555
No wonder that love is not always genuine. It is sometimes hatred disguised.   556

This is very common. One day one is held in high esteem, honored, praised.   557
The next, he is disparaged, denigrated, defamed. One is not at all surprised.   558

Don't be jubilant because you're raised to the top today, treated like a great hero.   559
If you do, you certainly will be desolate the day you're treated as nothing, a zero.   560

47

Do not ever crave to be famous. It's better for you to be obscure, i.e., incognito.   561
Because you'll never be or do all you want, but what the populace wants you to.   562

You may seem to be doing what you want; your freedom is restricted. You are in prison.   563
It is obvious that you committed no offence. That means you are punished for no reason.   564

You try, the best you can, to never judge,   565
And not hold against anyone a grudge.   566

Live in the here and now. But when you suffer and life in the present seems like hell,   567
You may live in the future and think of the happy days when you fully recover and heal.   568

Say no evil about anyone, you shall hear no evil spoken about you. What you hear is you echo.   569
The situation will not change, if you don't change your attitude, if you maintain the status quo.   570

Let no man fancy that because he is powerful and strong,   571
He can afford to do all he wants, whether right or wrong.   572

48

He ends in reclusion like Napoleon,   573
Or thrown into a cage like a lion.   574

For this reason, whether you live in a tent or a palace,   575
Avoid becoming popular lest you become populace.   576

People don't often sympathize with you. They may make your condition worse. It is of no avail   577
To say indiscriminately anything to them. You carefully choose what you can and can't reveal.   578

No matter how sick and weak you are, it is not to the point of losing honor and face.   579
However distressed or desolate you get, not to the point of losing hope and faith.   580

Even if you feel miserable, act as if you were happy. You will find   581
That by changing your behavior you'll be able to change your mind.   582

Whosoever shouts at you, you do not shout back,   583
Just as when a dog barks at you, you simply let it bark.   584

You don't even bother to tell him, "I heard you. Please stop."   585
Just as you deem of no use telling a dog "Be quiet. Shut up."   586

The best way to keep him quiet, when he shouts at you, is by silence.   587
If you shout back at him, he gets louder, as violence engenders violence.   588

Do not be agitated. Keep calm and serene, no matter the circumstance.   589
You sure will achieve inner peace not with denial but with acceptance.   590

When you say to people, 'Handle me with care. I am fragile. I am made of crystal',   591
They may do just the opposite. You must be strong as if you were made of metal.   592

Your interlocutor may think you are intelligent. If you tell him, 'Are you taking me for an idiot?'   593
He says 'No.' But deep inside he is convinced that's what you're, whether you admit it or not.   594

Many a person who is abused and treated by everyone all the time almost like an animal,   595
If you treat him/her kindly he/she thinks something's wrong with you. You are abnormal.   596

50

Choose very carefully your words before you talk. You'll be reminded of what you have said.   597
Just as you must be sure that what you will reap is what you want before planting a seed.   598

Some people with their deeds, good or bad, without knowing it, are writing history,   599
Which will sure be read by millions of people in every country, century after century.   600

Love yourself as you are. Don't rely on other people's estimation. Some may find you appealing   601
One time. Another time, in another place, the same or different people may find you appalling.   602

Many a time, when a human being is no longer oppressed, he or she reverses the roles.   603
He or she becomes the oppressor. He or she abuses and misuses everything he or she controls.   604

Instead of doing something to change things, we say there's nothing to do. That's human nature.   605
Yet, we must not accept it as *a fait accompli*. We must prevent that from happening in the future.   606

You watch a movie and you think for the first time, then you notice a scene,   607
Or hear a word, reminding you that it was a movie you've had already seen.   608

51

All we hear is "*marhaban*," welcome, peace be upon you, "*assalamu alaycome*." 609
But all we see is war waged by insensitive men, unconscious of tragic outcome. 610

All you hear is *assalamu alaycome*, peace be upon you. But all you see is war. 611
In other words, they say peace, but make war. They are unconscious, unaware. 612

You let no one take possession of what you have won, 613
What you have attained through an effort of your own. 614

You are a sensible human being, surely not to be treated like an immature adolescent. 615
"No one", says Eleanor Roosevelt, "can make you feel inferior without your consent." 616

You may suffer from different illnesses you cannot hide. But there may be stress 617
You prefer to keep to yourself, because it is something you are unable to express. 618

Do what you think is right with or without people's consent 619
Until you have got all your dues in full, a hundred per cent. 620

The food you think you are allergic to does not sicken you. It is your autosuggestion.   621
If you eat the same food without knowing it, you wouldn't likely have any indigestion.   622

It is not important whether or not you are rewarded when you do a good action.   623
You have already been sufficiently rewarded, drawing from it great satisfaction.   624

You go for so many years doing something, not realizing that you are making a big error,   625
Till you become aware seeing someone do the same, as if seeing yourself in the mirror.   626

Keep in mind there is no problem you can't solve or a difficulty you can't overcome.   627
All you have done, whether right or wrong, is the result of what you now have become.   628

You are mindful of yours actions and thoughts, good or bad. That is what makes you distinct   629
From other people who lead an unconscious life using not their intelligence but their instinct.   630

When someone says something that seems harsh, he may not mean to be rude.   631
Just as when he seems to be too interested in you, he may not mean to intrude.   632

We think we're free, but we are slaves, dominated not by the living but rather by the dead. 633

Whether we are guided in the right path or misled, we abide by what they said and did. 634

No matter how painful what you went or are going through, accept your fate. 635

It's not your fault. It's nobody's. Do your best to always be loving, never to hate. 636

Before you say something regretful, say it first to yourself and see how it would sound. 637

Yet saying something to yourself may be fine; to another, may be harmful, I have found. 638

It is not important how many years a man has lived. 639

What is important in a man's life is what he achieved. 640

When a man dies, people always ask, 'How long did he live?' 641

They never ask, 'How did he live? What did he achieve?' 642

"It's praiseworthy to live a long life." That's what people are always told. 643

They do not realize that some animal species also live and die very old. 644

To be loved by others and treated kindly you cannot expect   645
If you do not love yourself and if you have no self-respect.   646

You deserve to have the best of everything. You shall not accept anything cheap,   647
Neither will you let yourselves be driven to the pasture nor to the butchery like sheep.   648

You let no one put you down or lead you wherever he wants just like sheep.   649
From now on, you take charge of your life. You are the captain of your ship.   650

Being rich doesn't necessarily mean being generous. Similarly, being learned isn't sufficient.   651
What is important is being able to communicate one's knowledge, to be proficient, efficient.   652

Some people do nothing to improve themselves. There's no need to. They think they're perfect.   653
The lessons they could draw from other people's accomplishments have on them no effect.   654

You don't mind suffering if necessary, in order to be creative. Being creative is what you want.   655
Just like a seed, it cannot remain whole. It has to perish in order to give birth to a plant.   656

55

Man doesn't like to be told what to do. To make him do something is simple. 657
Like an ape, just do what you want it to, and then let it follow your example. 658

You can be loving, forgiving, tolerant; or the inverse. That is only a sample 659
Of what you can be. It is up to you to choose to be a good or a bad example. 660

Be cheerful, but avoid bad jokes, do not make unnecessary remarks, and so don't tease. 661
What you say may offend people instead of pleasing them and making them feel at ease. 662

Don't say anything indiscriminately to anyone, even if you are not serious, but only joking. 663
Because what may be funny in one culture, for another could be unpleasant, even shocking. 664

You think before you talk. What you say could be quite shocking, 665
Taken literally, even if you are not really serious but only joking. 666

The UN originally started as an idea and an ideal.   667

It is now striving not to end up as a deal and an ordeal.   668

With all the wars that are going on now in the world, is the UN still of great worth?   669

Yes, it is, there is no doubt about that. Without it, conditions would sure be worse.   670

Everybody feels pity for some sick writers who made their illness a national affair.   671
What about also caring for the millions of silent sick people? It would be very fair.   672

You may wonder, 'Who are these celebrities about whom people make a big fuss   673
When they only sneeze? When we get ill nobody cares about and thinks of us.'   674

58

All Nobel Peace Prize winners become famous, because they make a lot of noise.   675
What about those who strive for world peace silently and about whom nobody knows?   676

They certainly strive for peace for its own sake, not for getting any praise.   677
In other words, not for the sake of becoming famous and winning a prize.   678

Their concept of peace may be quite different. They stay at home. They don't go out   679
Into the street and demonstrate with the mob. They pray for peace. They don't shout.   680

They don't wish to become famous.   681
They choose to remain anonymous.   682

You ridicule no one, knowing that mocking others, it's yourself that you are mocking.   683
You would not distort your beautiful face by the grimaces you would be making.   684

When you walk and talk normally in the country of the lame and the stammerer, you are mocked.   685
They think that something is wrong with you and you're abnormal, strange. You are not shocked.   686

When you are assailed by bad memories, no matter how painful they are, do not dwell   687
On them. Instead of brooding over what makes you ill, focus on what makes you well.   688

Only when you stop searching, will you find what you seek.   689
As you start getting better, when you are sick of being sick.   690

You will do nothing for nobody's, but your own sake.   691
Whilst you remain altruistic, selfless, and give and take.   692

Henceforth, all we do, any action we undertake   693
Shall not be for anybody, but for our own sake.   694

You go on moving forward in confidence; you shall not slip.   695
However, open wide your eyes and look before you leap.   696

You won't do alone what you would be ashamed of doing before everyone. You do not hide. 697
You reveal everything unless it is a private matter. You are transparent, as inside so outside. 698

If you want no one to know what you are doing, do not do it. Sooner or later it will be known. 699
It is like hiding something under snow. When it melts, sooner or later it will be all shown. 700

Doing something foolish makes you wiser. You may have more to gain than to lose.   701
That doesn't mean it's all right to act foolishly; be careful next time; don't be too loose. 702

In other words, in not being mindful and acting foolishly, you may still have much to gain, 703
But not when someone else has to pick up the pieces. So, avoid acting the same way again. 704

Before saying and doing something, play it as a movie in you mind, sequence by sequence. 705
Imagining actually saying and doing it already enables you to foresee the consequence.   706

Sometimes you may feel so close to someone who is very far away, for instance. 707
As you may feel far from someone who's near you. It has nothing to do with distance. 708

When you undertake an action and you fail, try again till you succeed. Don't refrain 709
From acting for fear of making a mistake again. Dare to take risks. But use your brain. 710

We touch neither stone nor wood. 711
We think that wouldn't do us any bad or good. 712

Only because they wear a beard, they are ill shaven, they think they will be given, 713
Without having done anything for it, a free entry ticket to the kingdom of heaven. 714

Watching each one of them at his daily task, 715
One sometimes couldn't but wonder and ask: 716

'Are they the same persons seen praying in the church or the mosque?' 717
Yes, they sure are, but they can hardly be recognized, wearing a mask. 718

All yours sins are forgiven if, from now on, you will follow the right path.   719
Just as when you get dirty you wash, clean yourself by taking a good bath.   720

Whether they abstain or not from drinking wine,   721
Whether they eat or not kosher and/or swine,   722

That will not, in the Almighty's eyes, be all fine,   723
Nor will it make them any less or more divine.   724

For, on the Day of Judgment,   725
They sure will not be asked   726

What good food they have eaten,   727
But what good deeds they have done.   728

Be self-sufficient, self-reliant. Beware 729
Of borrowing. For you must be aware 730

He who loans you, 731
Owns you 732

He who saves you 733
Enslaves you. 734

He who feeds you 735
Starves you. 736

He who runs your affairs, 737
And rules over you, ruins you. 738

He who rescues you, if you are about to drown, 739
Has surely the power to sink you deep down. 740

He may not mean it, but just acts on a whim. 741
Therefore, you had better learn how to swim. 742

If you do not live up to his expectations,   743
If you do not defer to his wishes,   744

He who defends you,   745
Offends you.   746

He who nurtures you,   747
Tortures you.   748

He who loves you   749
Loathes you,   750

He who adores you,   751
Abhors you.   752

He who kisses, caresses you,   753
Curses you.   754

The crowds that shout today long live the President,   755
Will shout louder another day death to the President.   756

It is easier to kill a man than to convince him. 757
Or, it is harder to convince a man than to kill him. 758

When men fail to use the word, 759
They have recourse to the sword. 760

Then they give themselves the right to wage a war. 761
They know not what they're doing. They're unaware 762

Of the all the ruin, the harm, the damage 763
They cause others and their very self-image. 764

The civilized are the cause of all the ravages, 765
Absolutely not whom they label as savages. 766

They do all the slaughtering and killing afterward 767
That's done most of the time in the name of the Lord. 768

They expect to get for their deed a reward 769
In the hereafter, as well as in this world. 770

Instead of teaching the youngsters a skill, 771
They make out of them machines to kill. 772

66

You may not be able to perform miracles. 773

But you sure can overcome all obstacles. 774

When you get ill, let no one know about it. It may affect your health. Say nothing. Do not ever 775
Advertise it. People may keep on thinking of you as a sick person even when you fully recover. 776

You reap what you sow. 777

But that's not always so. 778

You plant a potato, 779

And reap a tomato. 780

To please a person you'd do all you could. 781

What you get in return may not be so good. 782

When someone is mad at you, he may take any good words you say to him as an insult. 783

To please him is to send him a kind t-mail.* That may be the only way to get good result. 784

(*) telepathic mail

67

Why do people seldom read photocopies? They can read them if they think they can. 785
They say they have no time. All photocopies are wasted. They end up in the trashcan. 786

One can tell how stingy or generous we are by the way we share what we have. 787
Just as it is so easy to know how bad or good we may be by the way we behave. 788

Happy and blessed are the destitute, the homeless and the vagabonds. 789
For they have nothing to lose, they have no attachments, no bonds. 790

People know when they lie to each other, 791
But they fool themselves and one another. 792

They tell lies without being ashamed, 793
Because they are ashamed to tell the truth. 794

Why do the things that have no meaning exist? 795
In order to give a meaning to those that do not exist. 796

If you tell me what your mother tongue is,   797
I can anticipate the mistakes you will make in Arabic.   798

In the same way, from the mistakes you make in Arabic,   799
I can tell you your mother tongue.   800

It's not important who says what. What's important is the saying not the sayer.   801
Just as a painting is appreciated for what it is worth, not depending on the seer.   802

Sometimes you hear something and you think it is the cause of your anger.   803
But what you hear has nothing to do with your reaction. It's only a trigger.   804

69

When you as a couple do care and really love each another,   805

You do not feel alone. Even apart, you are always together.   806

Man and woman are not one superior and another inferior. They complement each other.   807

Many a woman wrongly feels she is diminished, unless she gives birth and is a mother.   808

A woman has manifold missions right here in this life, on earth,   809

Other than being merely a good housewife, a mother, giving birth.   810

Men have brought the world into such a mess. All we see is hate, war and violence.   811

It is high time now for women to intervene to establish love, peace and benevolence.   812

Women are the majority. Therefore they should be the ruling class. That is democracy.   813

Men know that well but they say one thing and do another. Their policy is but a fallacy. 814

What you claim to be your own convictions, your thesis,   815
Are but what you were made to believe under hypnosis.   816

All that is said about some type of man,   817
Holds true for the same type of woman.   818

If a woman fails to seduce a man with her feminine charm,   819
She may simply leave him alone and not do him any harm,   820

Or get really violent and have recourse to a fatal arm.   821
Woe unto that unlucky man who lets her take his arm.   822

However, let's not dramatize things and give the alarm.   823
There is nothing to be upset about, and let's keep calm.   824

Men know very well that they owe their existence to women.   825
It is obvious, without women there would have been no men.   826

71

There is something mannish (1) in every woman. 827

As there is something womanish (2) in every man. 828

There is a little girl in every grown-up woman. 829

As there is a little boy in every grown-up man. 830

Our lives are sometimes run by our inner children by whom we are contaminated. 831

They've such a power over us. We can't resist them. We let ourselves dominated. 832

By observing closely very often the way you behave as an adult, 833

I can more or less accurately tell how you were raised as a child. 834

Conversely, if you reveal the ways you have been raised as a child, 835

I can somehow let you know how you would behave as a grown-up. 836

(1) Anima, Psychoanalysis Jung's term for the feminine part of a man's personality.
(2) Animus, Psychoanalysis Jung's term for the masculine part of a woman's personality.
ORIGIN Early 19th cent.: from Latin, 'spirit, 'soul'. (New Oxford Dictionary of English).

Whether you wear or not a veil,   837
That, for you, is really of no avail.   838

For what really matters,   839
Our dear beloved sisters,   840

Is not what you wear on your head,   841
But what you do bear in your heart.   842

You're ordered to cover yourselves as if you had something shameful to hide.   843
But you certainly do not. You are transparent. On the outside as on the inside. 844

What matters is your behavior, not your clothes. You wear what you think would suit.   845
It doesn't make a difference whether you wear a long or a short dress, a skirt or a suit.   846

Yet, if you wish to live in harmony with everyone, you ought to change your outfit,   847
As well as your very old ways of living. They are all outmoded. They no longer fit.   848

73

Just as you change your clothes if they no longer fit. 849
Because you gained a lot of weight and became fat. 850

Wherever you are, unite and free yourselves, Sisters. 851
You absolutely have nothing to lose but your fetters. 852

It makes really no difference at all whether you live in a tent or a castle. 853
What interests you is to be treated like a human being and not like cattle. 854

What is the use of going after you die to paradise, 855
If you're treated on this earth like merchandise? 856

In other words, what is really the use of having a good life in the far future, 857
If, in this very present moment, you are treated just like a piece of furniture. 858

Don't wait for anyone to give you your freedom. Don't be mistaken. 859
No one ever will. Be realistic. Freedom is never given; it is taken. 860

74

State your rights firmly, surely and clearly. Don't stutter. 861
You mustn't suffer today for a supposed happy life later. 862

Do not trade one for another; accept no bargain, no barter. 863
You need a decent life now and here, not in the hereafter. 864

You may be fortunate to get some outside help. 865
You certainly are required to take the first step. 866

Unless you act, your condition won't get any better. 867
No one can help you save yourselves in this matter. 868

You speak the same language, yet you can't communicate. 869
That is why you repress, hold everything in; you suffocate. 870

He does not treat you as a human being to educate; 871
He regards you as an animal to tame, to domesticate. 872

75

You are not fooled seeing a man kissing a woman's hand.　　873
Deep in his brain he may be kicking her, you understand.　　874

All he cares about is creating more goods for you to consume.　　875
That is the only thing he has in mind and thinks of, I presume.　　876

"You are attractive only if you use cosmetics and perfume."　　877
He is totally wrong, but that's what he makes you assume.　　878

Instead of just eating and drinking, and thus being merely a consumer, you must be a producer.　　879
Do not use cosmetics any longer, in order to be attractive. In other words, stop being a seducer.　　880

Their talk is all air and nonsense. Always remember this. Never forget.　　881
Bear in mind that everything you're promised is not what you will get.　　882

On hearing of all you are promised to get, you rejoice and exclaim, "How nice!"　　883
However, whether you get something at all or not, it must not come at any price.　　884

Whatever you do, it is not enough. You can never satisfy his ego.   885
Being co-dependent, if you want to leave him, he won't let you go.   886

With other men's wives, he behaves with all elegance,   887
Whereas with you, as his wife, he acts with arrogance.   888

He takes possession of everything you own   889
That you got through an effort of your own.   890

Do not take unnecessary risks, but "live dangerously."* Don't accept an easy life, 891
Doing little chores: cooking, cleaning, shopping and by merely being a housewife.   892

You made big progress in thought and in deed.   893
You surely have come a very long way indeed.   894

He seldom looks at or listens to you. That has been this way for years.   895
Sometimes you wonder what is the use for him to have eyes and ears.   896

(*) Nietzsche, Friedrich

77

There is no one to blame but himself, if he does something amiss.   897

As the Berber proverb goes, "He who hits himself does not miss."   898

You can no longer afford to be dependent and idle, you have to be active   899

To support yourselves in order to be free. You have no other alternative.   900

It may take a long time, but one day you sure will be free.   901

As a Chinese proverb says, "It takes ten years to grow a tree."   902

You're expected to be obedient, never to protest, and always say "Amen."   903

Whereas they are free to do and say all they want, because they are men.   904

Nearly each one of you is under tutelage all your life, treated like a child,   905

Not as a grown-up woman, and you're expected to be weak, meek and mild.   906

You may look outwardly big, strong, robust like an elephant,   907

But inwardly, you feel small weak, vulnerable like an infant.   908

He naively and wrongly thinks that you're submissive and obedient by nature. 909
That is why he is treating you with no consideration, like a piece of furniture. 910

He doesn't ask for your point of view. He wouldn't care less whether you consent or object. 911
Even though you are his partner, he regards you not as a human being but as an object. 912

It is nothing new. That has been the practice for centuries, 913
Not only where it originated but everywhere, in all countries. 914

He often makes you cry, but you do not recall him ever making you laugh. 915
He seldom tries to cheer you up. In all his behavior, he is rough and tough. 916

What is the use of showering you with jewelry, candy? 917
What you need most from him is to be treated kindly. 918

From men's point of view, you should consider yourselves very lucky, 919
Because they treat you simply as a half human being, not as a monkey. 920

There is nothing to learn from him. All he wants to teach you, you already knew.   921

It is always the same story. You have heard it a hundred times. It is nothing new   922

In the court of justice, a convict may have a single man to witness on his behalf,   923

Or two women,(1) for a woman is regarded not as a full human being but as a half.   924

In a more or less similar situation, for instance,   925

A man gets two women's share of inheritance.(2)   926

Men are advised to reprove and beat women if they don't obey   927

But to leave them alone, if they follow the rules and abide by.(3)   928

Assert yourself as a full human being as long as you live.   929

For you are held as a half human being! Hard to conceive.   930

But that is what you, for centuries, were made to believe.   931

You are intelligent. How could you be so easy to deceive?   932

(1) "And get two witnesses, out of your own men. And if there are not two men, then a man and two women." Quran, 2:282.
(2) "As regards your children's (inheritance) to the male a portion equal to that of two females," Quran 4:11.
(3) "... beat them; but if they return to obedience, seek not against them means (of annoyance)..." Quran, 4:34.

Even if you take part in worldly things, you live like a nun   933
In a convent. You're not supposed to enjoy life and have fun.   934

You have been suffering for a very long time without consolation.   935
From now on, you can be subjected to no more harm and tribulation.   936

If any of you has a feeling of nausea, and gets a sense of vertigo,   937
That's because of the ill treatment you constantly have to undergo.   938

He could do all sorts of things good and bad for you, without you being consulted.   939
When you do something for yourself, without asking his consent he feels insulted.   940

He bores you so, always repeating the same discourse.   941
It is never his fault; you get all the blame and the curse.   942

All you can do is let things take their own course.   943
Being wise, you don't want to make things worse.   944

He is lost without you; you are his whole life, his source. 945

He wants you, altogether, as a wife, a maid and a nurse. 946

He regards you just as a plaything, a precious toy 947

He holds for a while with great pleasure and joy. 948

Then this pleasure ends, you are but a nuisance to destroy. 949

Thus behaving immaturely, like a brat, a little spoiled boy. 950

He may fancy being Paris (a Trojan prince), and you his Helen of Troy. 951

And after having written a small book, he identifies himself with Tolstoy. 952

He does not take you seriously when you speak solemnly. All he does is laugh. 953

When you behave the same way he does, he understands that enough is enough. 954

He always says unpleasant things to hurt your feelings, to make you cry. 955

But he says nothing to make you laugh, feel good. He wouldn't even try. 956

82

Everything is possible. You can have access to anything you yearn for. Everything is within your reach. 957
You can do everything man has thus far monopolized. You can be knowledgeable and rich. 958

The acts of violence you're confronting daily abound. 959
You can neither act nor react; you are religion-bound. 960

Whether you are with him or not on common ground, 961
Whether you progress or just go round and round, 962

Whether you stay put or are free to move around, 963
Whether you are free to go out or are house-bound, 964

Physically and/or psychologically you are held hostage 965
By the family, religion, society, your whole entourage. 966
All your endeavors of liberation are met with sabotage. 967

You cannot express yourselves or make any comment. 968

All you can afford to do is mourn, wail and lament. 969

All these are causes of your distress and torment. 970

However you excel yourself, he pays you no compliment. 971

You interest him merely for use as a tool, an instrument. 972

He is unstable; he may act in any manner, any moment. 973

You cannot discuss with him; he accepts no argument. 974

You had no formal education. You have no degree because you didn't go to college. 975

That is quite all right. Nobody and nothing prevents you from acquiring knowledge. 976

You can study by yourself, acquire more knowledge and become a very learned lady. 977

You don't have to be taught anything by anyone, nor go to university and get a Ph.D. 978

84

You may not know much about him; he is almost like a stranger.   979

For this reason, he may frighten you, as if you were facing danger.   980

You are not allowed to associate and mingle.   981

You are constantly put in a hopeless tangle.   982

Considering the matter from a humane angle,   983

No matter how bravely and hard you struggle,   984

Regardless of whether you are married or single,   985

You can do nothing against the law of the jungle.   986

Whether as a daughter, a sister, a mother or a wife,   987

You often are involved with him in perpetual strife.   988

However plainly trying to explain to him, it's all the same.   989

He boldly thinks, you're, for everything, the one to blame.   990

One can tell very quickly who he's, by him using slang,   991

And telling bad jokes, as well as by slips of the tongue,   992

Relating unbelievable stories that are all hard to swallow.   993

The funny thing is that he could be a highly educated fellow,   994

A Ph.D., a professor of philosophy or of international law.   995

He thinks he's perfect, not admitting having one single flaw.   996

Whoever does something wrong you're the one to scold.   997

He believes you're the one who never do as you're told.   998

Be happy and rejoice, for, to your most advantage,   999

The whole situation will, for sure, radically change.   1000

You finally will be delivered from the male bondage,   1001

Get rid once and for all of the burden of past heritage.   1002

Whether you are homebound or not, your freedom is restricted. You are in prison.   1003
It's obvious you committed no offence. That means you are punished for no reason.   1004

Some men of all ranks tend to be alike. "As above, so below."   1005
Whatever one of them undertakes, him do all others follow.   1006

Whatever his standing and social status, be it high or low.   1007
He swims against the current instead of going with the flow.   1008

He comes to his senses, when he experiences a hammer blow   1009
He takes all his time when dealing with him, being too slow.   1010

Yet he wants everyone he is dealing with to be very hasty.   1011
Or else he loses his temper and suddenly turns very nasty.   1012

You shall not let yourself be tricked, like Eve, by a snake.   1013
That's why you mustn't sleep, but be always wide-awake.   1014

You were born an eagle, but he made you believe, by repeating, for centuries time and again,   1015
That you're but a chicken. You succumbed. To keep you under control, he had everything to gain.   1016

Though carried and nourished for nine months in their abdomen,   1017
Some men still have no scruples regarding women as a bad omen   1018

Yet, men are not all alike. They do not all think and act the same way. Let us bear in mind   1019
That they are not all monstrous. Let's not be mistaken. Many of them are gentle and kind.   1020

All men and women are held in the same respect.   1021
They're alike. They're neither very bad nor perfect.   1022

There are men and women on whom you can rely.   1023
They are reliable and trustworthy. They do not lie.   1024

Both marvelous and wonderful men and women exist, and are not hard to find.   1025
They may only be a minority, an elite, and the *crème de la crème* of mankind.   1026

88

If I were a religious person: a Muslim, a Christian or a Jew,   1027

How would I pray and worship God, in your point of view?   1028

How would I worship God?   1029

I would worship Him by doing good   1030

and abstaining from doing evil,   1031

and also by silent prayers.   1032

Thus I do not have to devote any place   1033

or time to worship and devotion   1034

during the week, the day or at night,   1035

being in a state of worship and devotion   1036

everywhere and all the time,   1037

throughout the week, day and night.   1038

For it is only my behavior in everyday existence,   1039

the way I live each minute, each hour,   1040

the right I do, the wrong I abstain from doing, that counts.   1041

In other words, what really counts   1042

is not observing the Sabbath,   1043

going to church every Sunday,   1044

nor praying five times a day,   1045

that make me righteous, virtuous, pious,   1046

but what I do and the way I behave in between,   1047

all day long and throughout the week   1048

What is my profession?   1049
My profession is...   1050
Does it really matter what my profession is?   1051
In other words, does it make a difference   1052
Whether I earn my living as   1053
a janitor or as a senator?   1054
What I do for a living is of no importance.   1055
It is what I do live for that should be of   1056
importance and must have a meaning,   1057
being concerned more about the sense,   1058
the meaning, than about the means of living.   1059

Jesus Christ was a carpenter,   1060
Socrates a stone-cutter,   1061
Joan of Arc an uneducated peasant-girl.   1062
But they are not known to History   1063
as carpenter, stone-cutter and   1064
uneducated peasant-girl, respectively.   1065
In other words, they are   1066
certainly not known to History   1067
for what they did for a living,   1068
but, first and foremost,   1069
for what they did live and die for!   1070

✳

90

Index

Index

Index

Index

Index

Index